Computers
Are Easy to Understand

I0004892

Wikipedia - Jared C Benedict

i

This book is written in "Mosaic Style." The brief words - like puzzle pieces - fit together to make a complete picture of computers.

Table of Contents

Page	Description
1	Intro
3	Data Patterns
5	On and Off e-Pulses
7	Chips – Up Close
9	L-Patterns and Pixels
11	Memory Magnets
13	Dots and Blots on Paper
14	Inkjet
16	Laserjet
19	Computer Connections
21	Lines and Lives that Inter-Link
24	More
25	USB Drive e-pulses
27	CD / DVD - Light Patterns
29	Cell Phone - Radio Waves
31	Not Very Mobile Phones
32	Integrated World

Computers are all around us.
They look complicated but the
basics are easy to understand.

1

Computers are part of the patterns of our daily lives. Let's look at the patterns of how computers work.

2

Data is made up of patterns of information. These patterns change from one form of power to another.

As an example, in a telephone, our voice changes into patterns of electricity and then back into sound.

Computers work with patterns of electricity, light and magnets? Let's focus first on e-pulses of electrical patterns.

Wikipedia by Deasington

Wikipedia by Tomomarusan

Wikipedia - Public Domain

4

When we flip a light switch, we turn electricity on and off. Computers switch electricity on and off billions of times a second. Now you know part of the secret of how computers work. Tiny pulses of on or off electricity, we call e-pulses, make patterns that represent data. Before a computer will work, all data must be changed into on or off e-pulses.

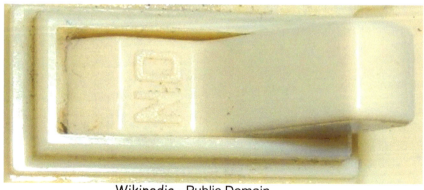

For example, the letter "A" is the e-pulses: off-on-off-off-off-off-off-on. In computer code, it is written as:

0 1 0 0 0 0 0 1.

One mean the electricity is on. Zero means it is off. The word "digital" means data that is made of patterns of 1's and 0's. Digital is the basic language of computers. Pushing a keyboard letter or number key, sends a pattern of e-pulses to the chip, also called a microprocessor. This chip is the brains of a computer.

Look at a chip up close. It is full of lines and logic links. There are paths and processes. The e-pulses race along thin lines like cars on a super highway. Logic is the way digital data flows through the chip.

 The microprocessor chip is called a CPU or Central Processing Unit. The CPU uses directions to turn on and off tiny switches [called transistors] like traffic lights, to control the flow of e-pulses of data. These instructions are called software. Software controls the flow of data through a computer. It turns individual letters into e-mails and separate numbers into balanced checkbooks. The CPU sends e-pulses to the computer screen.

The first chip had a couple of thousand transistors. Today, chips have over a billion transistors.

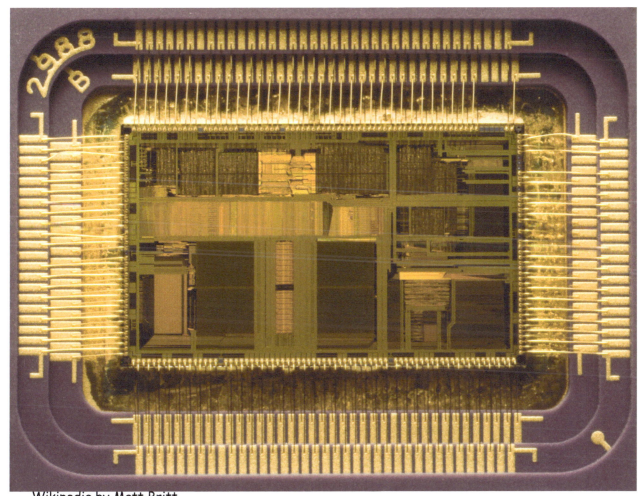

The Microprocessor chip is called
a CPU – Central Processing Unit.

8

The e-pulses change into points of light that make the screen glow. Each point of light is called a pixel. Each pixel has a red, green and blue part. Everything we see on the screen is made of patterns of light. We call them I-patterns of pixels. That is, all the colors we see on the screen are actually tiny patterns of three colors of dots. The screen shows us what we are creating on the computer. The actual data is stored in the computer's memory.

Wikipedia

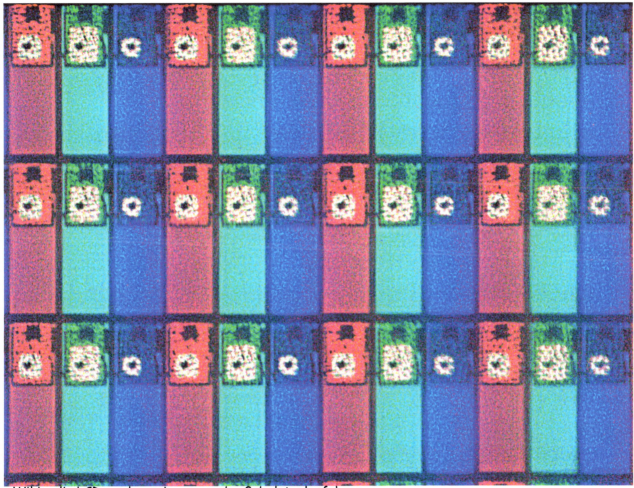

Wikipedia LCD_under_microscope by Gabelstaplerfahrer

10

The e-pulses change into patterns of micro-magnets in the computer's memory There are two types of computer memory: short and long term. The on and off e-pulses go from the CPU chip to computer's short term memory. This Memory changes the e-pulses into patterns of on or off micro-magnets or m-patterns. The m-patterns are temporarily stored for quick use by the computer. The m-patterns can be quickly converted back to e-pulses. The e-pulses are also saved as on or off m-patterns into long term memory called disk drives. What we create on a computer can also be printed.

Wikipedia by Aney

12

Printers use ink dots or blots to make patterns. There are two types of printers: inkjet and laserjet.

Wikipedia by Combuchan

Wikipedia

13

For Inject Printers, the e-pulses are turned into tiny dots of ink. Thousands of dots per inch are put quickly onto the paper.

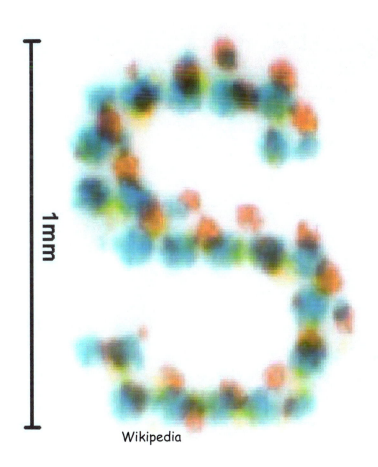

1mm

S

Wikipedia

This is how to inkjet print.
Data comes from the computer.
1) chips send directions
that 2) scroll the paper

and 3) readies the ink
4) jets print tiny dots
onto the paper.
5) loads the next paper

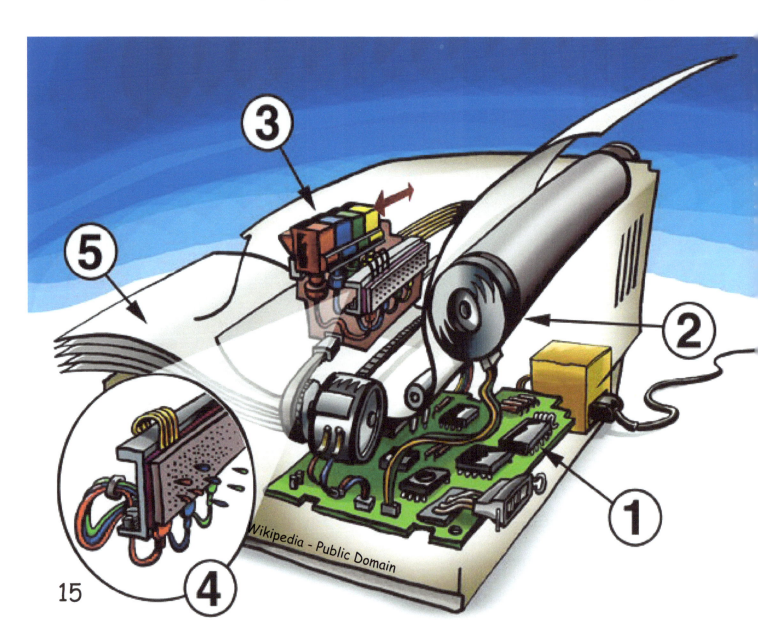

Wikipedia - Public Domain

15

For laserjet printers, e-pulses change into light patterns that shine on a drum. The drum is covered with micro electrical charges. The laser draws patterns on the drum.

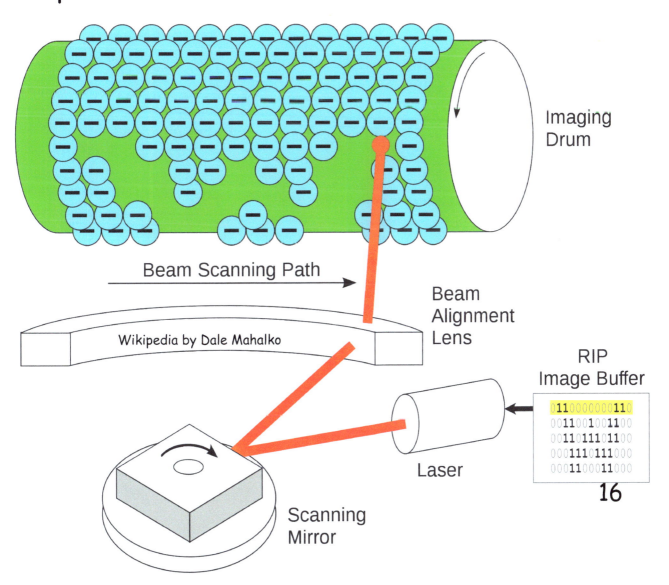

Imaging Drum

Beam Scanning Path

Beam Alignment Lens

Wikipedia by Dale Mahalko

RIP Image Buffer

0110000000110
00110010001100
00110111011100
00011101111000
00011100011000

Laser

16

Scanning Mirror

The remaining e-charges pick up dots of ink and then blot them onto paper. The ink, called toner is heated so it sticks to the paper.

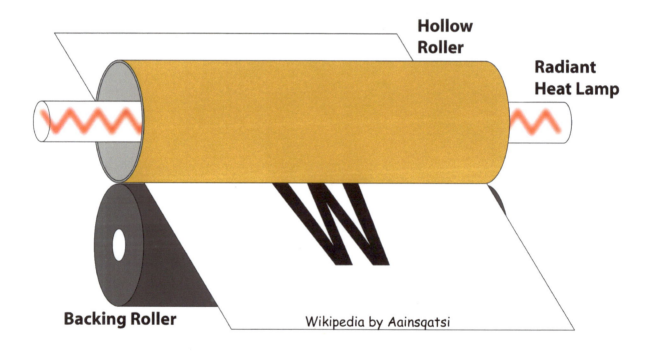

Hollow Roller

Radiant Heat Lamp

Backing Roller

Wikipedia by Aainsqatsi

Single pages join into books and books become libraries. Similarly, there is a need to connect separate computers.

18

Individual computers are
connected into a network
called The Internet. It links
separate computers from around
the world together. The "web"
is the name for the text and
images that people create.

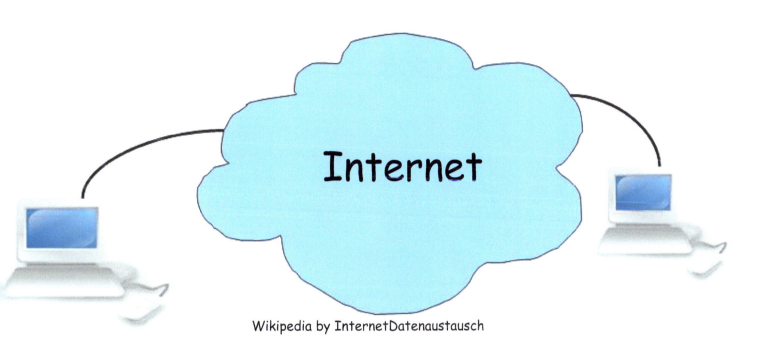

Internet

Wikipedia by InternetDatenaustausch

20

If you draw a picture of the network lines that connect our planet, the patterns look much like the integrated circuits of the computer's brain chip. The lines all inter-link.

21

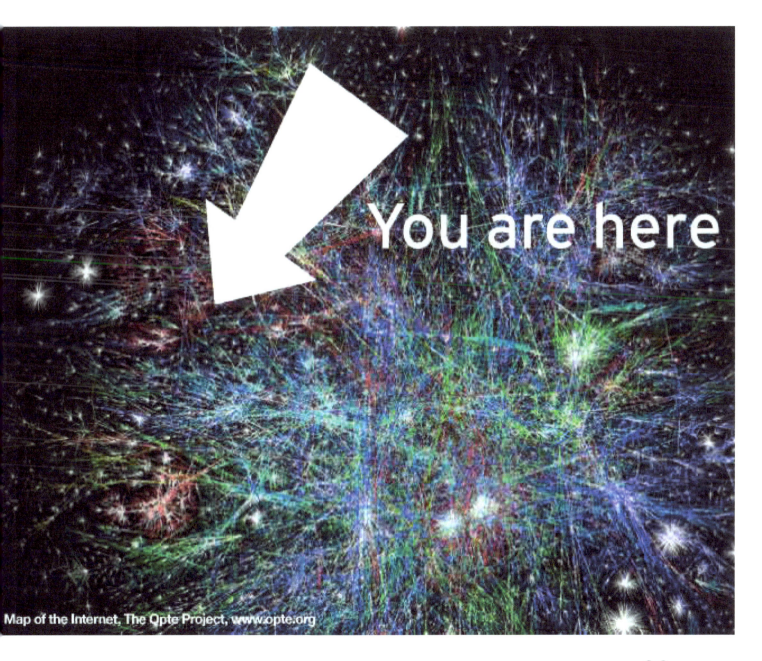

Map of the Internet, The Opte Project, www.opte.org

How do computers work? The e-pulses flow in chips; lights glow on the screen and magnets stow memories. The different computer parts integrate together to make a computer work. The separate computers connect together to make the internet and world-wide web. Interconnected computers provide open access to much of the world's knowledge. May we inter-weave the data into wisdom that leads to global peace and prosperity.

For those who
want to know more
about computers.

USB DRIVE

This is a USB Drive
That e-pulses enter
That change into e-charges
(like static electricity)
That are stored in chips
That change back into e-pulses
And are read by a computer

Compact Disc (CD)

This is a CD
That has micro-bumps
That bounce light into a sensor
That turns them into e-pulses
That computers use
And CD Players too.

The micro-bumps or no bumps represent digital 0's and 1's.
Writable CD's have a special light sensitive coating. The
laser burns bumps or no bumps to write 1's and 0's to the
disc. DVD's work in similar ways to the CD's

CD Player

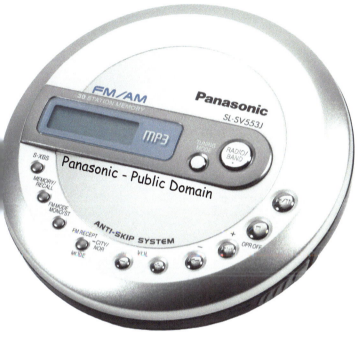

Wikipedia by Arun Kulshreshtha

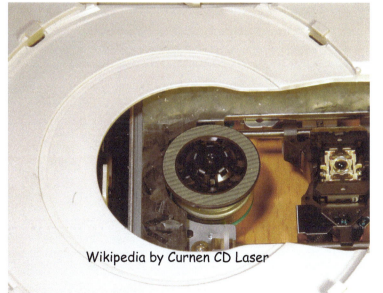

Wikipedia by Curnen CD Laser

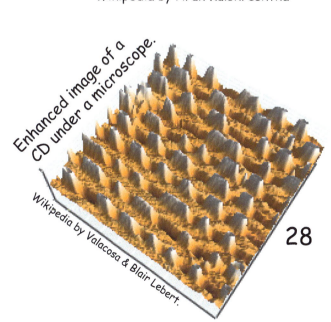

Enhanced image of a CD under a microscope.

Wikipedia by Valacosa & Blair Lebert.

28

Cell Phone

This is a cell phone
That sounds enter
That are changed into e-pulses
and next into radio waves
That make their way to the other phone
Where radio waves enter the antenna
That are then changed into e-pulses
That are turned into sounds
That are patterns of the speakers voice

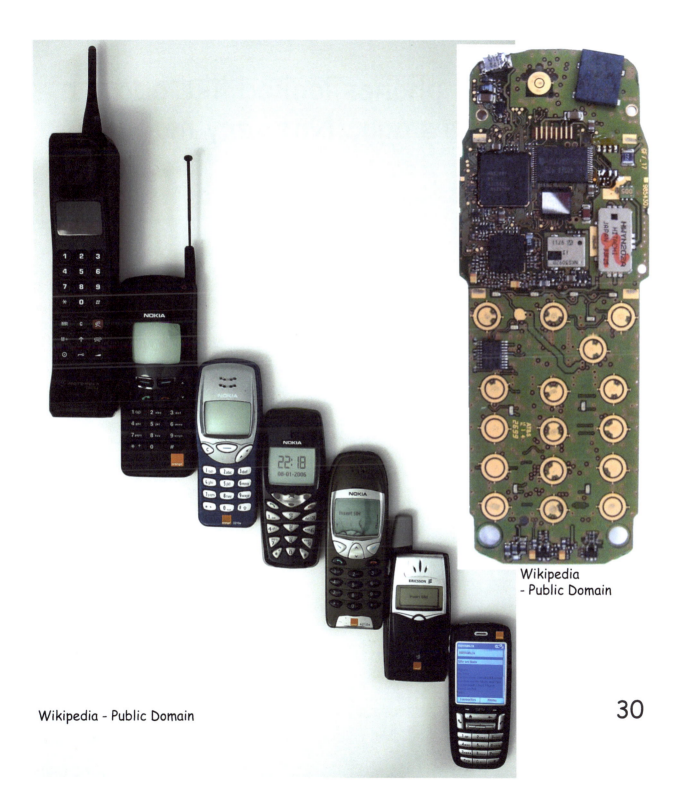

Wikipedia
- Public Domain

Wikipedia - Public Domain

30

This is what phones looked like about a hundred years ago. Not very mobile.

31

Integrated chips enable the modern age of computers. The lines link circuits, networks and lives. We hope that easier global communication will lead to greater understanding.

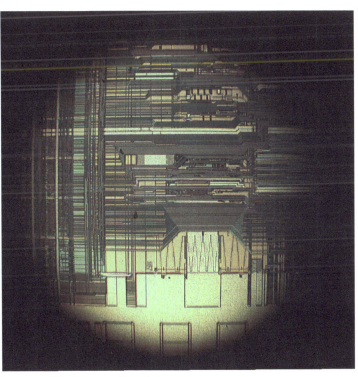

Wikipedia Intel 80486 Chip by Uberpenguin

Credits

Unless otherwise noted, pictures are part of the public domain

We would like to thank:

www.wikipedia.com

The Intel Museum (www.intel.com)

Computer History Museum (www.computerhistory.org)

Buy Our Other Books:

All Are Equal – From Slavery to Civil Rights
Ant City – Mot and the Think Center
Big Die – Earth's Mass Extinctions
Billy Bee's Big Sneeze – Overcome Obstacles
Brit Mu Briefly - From Seeds to Civilization
Catch Phrase Come-Froms - Origins of Idioms
Chase to Space – The Space Race Story
Civil Sense – What if There Wasn't a Civil War?
Common Come-Froms – Origins of Objects
Computer Patterns – A Ditty on Digital
Computers: Count, Compute & Connect
Cozy Clozy – From Fibers to Fabrics
Different Words – Same Meaning
Essence of America – The I's in US
Essence of Science – 7 Eye Opening Ideas
Fishi and Birdy - A Fable of Friends
6 Chicken & 5 K's - The Thai Alphabet
How Do Hedgehogs Hug? - Many Ways to Show Love
Humi Bird - A Humble Tale
Images in Action - Why Movies Move
Jungle Fire - Flee or Fix
Meaning of Money - The American Way
Nature's Links of Life
Ogs, Zogs & Useful Cogs – A Tale of Teamwork
Paintings With Insects, Eggs & Oils – An Intro to Art
Queen Jeen - And The Thrown Throne
Robin's First Flight – Wings of Courage
Shoe Walks – With Funky Fairy
Sky-Lings: An Intro to Airplanes
Space Port: Maps to Mars
Stars of Days & Months – The Story of 7 and 12
Sun's Above the Clouds – A Sunny Point of View
Turtle Jumps - A Tale of Determination
Where Cookies Come-From - From Dough to Delicious
Who Did What in World History? Past Echoes in the Present
Why is California Interesting? – Dreams of Gold
Why is England Interesting? – Worldwide Words
Why is Thailand Interesting? – Source of the Smiles
Why is the USA Interesting? - The 50 State Quarters
Yo Frog – The Surprising Songs

Books are also available at http://www.amazon.com
Please contact us at: trythaiketco@gmail.com

Recommended further reading:

Computers
Count, Compute & Connect

Douglas J. and Pakaket Alford